D0800699

This book was made possible
by the generous support of the Estate of EMK

Books by Michael Waters

Bountiful
The Burden Lifters
Anniversary of the Air
Not Just Any Death
Fish Light

Dissolve to Island: On the Poetry of John Logan (Ed.)

OCLC
12.50
#36721276

Green Ash, Red Maple, Black Gum

New Poems by

MICHAEL WATERS

811
W331g

BOA Editions, Ltd. ꙮ Rochester, NY ꙮ 1997

East Baton Rouge Parish Library
Baton Rouge, Louisiana

Copyright © 1997 by Michael Waters
All rights reserved

LC #: 96–86390
ISBN: 1–880238–42–X cloth
ISBN 1–880238–43–8 paper

First Edition
97 98 99 00   7 6 5 4 3 2 1

Publications by BOA Editions, Ltd.—
a not-for-profit corporation under section 501 (c) (3)
of the United States Internal Revenue Code—
are made possible with the assistance of grants from
the Literature Program of the New York State Council on the Arts,
the Literature Program of the National Endowment for the Arts,
the Lannan Foundation, the Sonia Raiziss Giop Charitable Foundation,
the Eric Mathieu King Fund of The Academy of American Poets,
as well as from the Rochester Area Foundation Community Arts Fund
administered by the Arts & Cultural Council for Greater Rochester,
the County of Monroe, NY,
and from many individual supporters.

Cover Design: Daphne Poulin-Stofer
Cover Painting: e. e. cummings
Author Photo: Rick Maloof
Typesetting: Richard Foerster
Printed in Canada by Best Book Manufacturers
BOA Logo: Mirko

BOA Editions, Ltd.
A. Poulin, Jr., President
(1938–1996)
260 East Avenue
Rochester, NY 14604

CONTENTS

In Memory of My Father

Raymond Waters

Who invented the human heart, I wonder? Tell me, and then show me the place where he was hanged.

—Lawrence Durrell
Justine

Green Ash, Red Maple, Black Gum

GREEN ASH, RED MAPLE, BLACK GUM

How often the names of trees consoled me,
how I would repeat to myself *green ash*
while the marriage smouldered in the not-talking,
red maple when the less-than-tenderness flashed,
then *black gum, black gum* as I lay next to you
in the not-sleeping, in the not-lovemaking.

Those days I tramped the morass of the preserve,
ancient ash smudging shadows on stagnant pools,
the few wintry souls skulking abandoned wharves.
In my notebook I copied plaques
screwed to bark, sketching the trunks' scission,
a minor Audubon bearing loneliness like a rucksack.

And did the trees assume a deeper silence?
Did their gravity and burl and centuries-old patience
dignify this country, our sorrow?

So as I lay there, the roof bursting with invisible
branches, the darkness doubling in their shade,
the accusations turning truths in the not-loving,
green ash, red maple, black gum, I prayed,
in the never-been-faithful, in the don't-touch-me,
in the can't-bear-it-any-longer,
black gum, black gum, black gum.

TWO BATHS

One

Lovelier than Susannah
who set the elders' hearts groaning at twice their faithful
stride, so that each grandfather
clutched his breast to remember the beauty of the nude
female body, you tilted
the pail to plash well-water over stepped terraces
of flame-red hair, rivulets
snaking down breasts, God-thumbed birth-stain, vulval thatch
    and thighs.
And I lavished the shampoo
as you knelt in the rue anemone, spiraea's
windfall stippling burnished skin,
lather foaming through my fingers, foaming shut your eyes
as you took me in your mouth,
the sun bearing witness to our blind, intuitive
coupling, till I tipped the pail
to rinse our fallen flesh, let our imperfections glisten.

Two

Light roused us from the depths of our separate longings
and while I balanced buckets
you laced black sneakers for your morning run on the cliff,
wrapped the red ribbon of shirt
around your forehead, stretched stiff calf muscles, then ran off.
I could see you jog the beach
as I arranged notebooks, pens, on the marble table,
then begin the zigzagging
goat-path toward the crag overlooking our stone cottage,
your red rag still visible
against the rough, anaemic marble of the mountain.
Remember the undressing,
how I slipped off your Nikes, peeled each slick of cotton,
then unknotted the sweatband
and dipped that tatter into the icy water, sponge
pressed between your breasts, your legs,
the tenderness between us before the sex turned sour?—
before your six miles became
a more-than-tacit withdrawal, like sleep, or headphoned jazz,
so I'd watch you crest the hill
as I worked at the marble table, wrenching lines, syl-
lables, the diminishing
sweatband a raw wound in the distance, as I revised
draft after draft, prodding you
past the horizon, writing you out of existence.

AIRING THE MATTRESS

Ios

How each stain wept into another—semen,
saliva—, the bodily fluids of the sick
smudged by rainwater, the green-black
molds of winter flourishing, then fading, till
a color never named, *loss* or *desire*, slicked over
the warp of the mattress, seeped into straw
ticking, so the mattress exhaled
its sodden history each evening.
Dawns we propped it against one ash withered by wind,
let the salt-stewed vapors sweep, molecule
by molecule, into the vaster currents
as pale watermarks burned legible,
eros & misery etched over cotton crevasses,
our impress upon the mattress the record
of our lives' impulse toward wreckage
for future lovers to decipher, then
struggle to transcend, as we struggled, those nights
after drying the mattress, after hauling it
back into the stone cottage where we lay
sleepless in the downward spiral of stars
& rain & perpetual need, helpless not to deepen
the archetypal, sex-struck stain,
helpless not to blend
our human bodies till we bleed.

PARTHENOPI

Ios

Once we beheld the brilliance of our estate
reflected in the haloed serenity of the girl
who prepared the basketful of cucumbers for salad,
slicing each nub into watery wheels,
columns of coins in the egg-white bowl.
Then she'd lift each miniature transparency
as she'd seen the priest flourish the Host,
thumb the serrated blade
to nick the green, then twist her wrist
to peel back the dust-plumed skin, the rubbery shavings
heaping a wild garden, unspoiled Eden, on the wooden counter.
Again and again she consecrated each wafer.
We basked in her patience, that rapt transportation,
her bell-shaped, narrowing eyelids as she spun
one papery sun, then the next, her perfect happiness,
smoke from the blackened grillwork wreathing her hair,
the fat of the slaughtered lamb hissing in the fire.
Her name—we'd asked our waiter—was Parthenopi, "little virgin."
We were still a couple then, our summer's lazy
task to gather anecdotes toward one future,
each shared and touching particular
to be recited over baked brie and chilled chardonnay
in the grasp of some furious, if distant, winter.
"Parthenopi," one of us might say, chiming a glass,
but the common measure of love is loss.
The cucumbers glistened in oil and thyme.

17

GOD AT FORTY

I think God must be reading,
or crumpling love letters, or poking His cramped finger
into the ash of the dead
fire to resurrect the flames and warm His mildewed room.
Rain spatters the cabin roof.
One hushed breeze freshens the crab apple blossoms upstate
where God summers. They're pleasant,
these evenings spent in solitude, though God remembers
each of His former lovers
who steamed exotic meals for wary angels, Thai oil
to relieve the strict boredom
of living with a brooding Being whose creative pulse
drove Him inward, whose silence—
that dour guest—too often graced their bountiful table.
Now God keeps His meals simple,
noodle soup simmered on the single coil, peppered brie
slabbed on chunks of broken bread.
Late afternoons neighbors bring baskets of blueberries,
predict dry weather, then leave.
Near dusk God revises His poems, counting syllables—
traditional forms soothe Him
(though He prefers free verse), lend emotional restraint,
keep Him from stepping over
the border of sentimentality where minor
post-modernists stray. Not God.
His eyes water, the owl's clawed feet loose the poplar branch,
the fire wavers, and He sleeps.
Another shitty day in paradise, He might joke
on scrawled postcards never sent.
And dreams: unclasped bra, sunburnt back, freckled skin peeling.
Ants file the smoke-smudged ceiling.
One mouse scurries from its woodpile shelter, zigzags back.

Then God awakens, opens
His black binder to erase some easy metaphor.
He never answers prayers, but
heeds His morning routine: NPR, knee-bends, java,
then work, always the work, lost
for hours in rough drafts, until the broth boils, the cheese wedge
flicks its furred green tongue of mold,
or the last loaf crumbles, and God's immense loneliness
overwhelms. He scrapes His pocked,
bristly cheek along the splinter-shot table, eyes shut,
allowing His vast yearning
to wash over the planet, cool scouring blankness, that
leaf-lit, resplendent seepage
whose source He sometimes forgets—within Him or without?
Rain quickens the white dwarf pines.
God's manuscript blows open, thumbed leaves riffling, their chirr
the psalm of His rasped breathing.

SWAMP ROSE MALLOW

Hibiscus palustris

Because they loomed as large as Salvation
Army tubists, their ruffled buds vaguely
Victorian, pink blooms waggling churchgoers'

tongues, we felt as though we were not alone;
still we touched and pressed our rabbity lengths
and might have undressed ourselves utterly,

except for their sober, swaying patience.
So we plucked one we could reach from the rail
of the wooden path, knowing we shouldn't,

bore its flushed bloom miles back to our bedroom,
tossing that frail witness among the stained
rumples, then fucked. I teased those plush petals

along the swollen lips of your vulva
as you murmured *soft, so soft!* . . . then held you
as you trembled once more. Then once more. Then

you floated that stunned flower in a perse
earthenware bowl to allow its blatant,
sexual odor to disseminate

across the scrubbed sprawl of suburbia,
loosing its gamey surge and miasmal
vapors beyond chalked macadam and tile

to rouse the Sunday shoppers at the mall.

EVERLASTING PEA

Lathyrus latifolius

The smoky aroma of Lapsang souchong
garlands the deck; false butterflies assume
their wild, argentine & crimson blooms:

déjà vu: the cool silence of our room:
the river slipping light through latticed windows;
the upper branches of silver birches

not yet awash with thrushsong;
when we touched along the flared lengths of our limbs,
igniting one moment of that slow, Connecticut summer

—dawn's hazy blue Twachtmanian landscape—,
we assumed our habitation among the everlasting,
their swollen, sensual beauty always

on the verge of flight, almost
apart from creeping leaf and tendril, almost
another trick of the light. But that silence:

that *something-about-to-happen*: how
we startled it by reading aloud
the letters of Rupert Brooke to Cathleen Nesbitt:
"Could a thousand poems repay God for your mouth?"

NEW AGE

The Sunday I blew sixty dollars on a taxi
just to break away from you,
the New Age driver, eyeing me—wild-haired, reeking sex—
turned Mr. Solicitous,
asking me to "share" (the name of that skinny actress)
the deep source of my distress.
No. Blessed silence. "Relationship," he flashed turquoise.
I ached to yank his hooped hair.
("Under every ponytail," my father once told me
—big grin—"there's a horse's ass.")
"I knew a woman once," he twirled the stud in one lobe.
"We fought like blind billy goats.
If they can't accept you for what you are . . ." he trailed off,
such vast wisdom too weighty
to articulate fully as we throttled along
the wavering interstate.
At Tweed-New Haven, I fumbled him three twenties, slapped
thirty-five on the counter
to revise my Super Saver, then slumped on a graf-
fitied bench. Soon I grew calm.
Three hours till the next flight home. The vacant terminal
commenced its tidy business.
A pay phone shrilled, Car Rental answered, then hustled off.
Maintenance swept by, puzzled
the swaying receiver, hung up. Ramon— red name stitched
on oil-spattered coveralls—
slow-poked over sip by sip, careful not to wobble
his styrofoam cup—the steam
stubbling his chin with thin ranks of angelic orders—,
gazed along the uniform
bank of phones, then shrugged away. Somewhere evolution
had begun its sharp descent.

I hefted my romance, tattered *Pan* by Knut Hamsun:

> *'I am depressed and full of sad thoughts tonight,'* I say.
> *And in her sympathy she makes no answer.*
> *'I love three things,'* I say then. *'I love a dream of love I*
> *once had, I love you, and I love this patch of earth.'*
> *'And which do you love best?'*
> *'The dream.'*

The dream. Ninety-five bucks. Hmm.
I sifted some coins, dialed, asked you please to come get me.
How many unnameable
passions must we ruin till we hurt each other enough?
How many grievances mouth
till the splintery soul flames beyond resurrection?
Let the ambiguities
of fiction conspire complex answers. All you required,
love, was a little change.

SIMPLE HAPPINESS

You have done too much of the exquisite,
Henry James consoled Whistler, *not to have earned*
more despair than anything else.
You have sponged the storm windows
and raised them, then lowered summer's screens
to allow the feathery brume of pollen
to sweep into your room. And you have stepped,
barefoot, across the muffled wooden slats,
trailing footprints from the bed to the shower
where you smoothed the green oval of soap
over your arms and breasts and belly,
let the sulfurous waters jet
the pollen from your hair till the foam
swirling into the basin burst
bright yellow. And you have shaken open the towel
from the wicker basket to buff your coral
body dry, then sprinkled powder onto one palm,
small puffs burgeoning the swollen layers of air.
I sit at my table imagining your morning,
the pollen that pummeled your flesh
tumbling room to room till blown across rooftops
to sift down into soft heaps around me, infinitesimal
stars signaling the explosion of one galaxy
and the slow, laborious creation of the next,
and by now you have pressed your face
into the faded flowers of your dress,
remembering that passage I read to you,
Svevo in a letter to his beloved Livia:
. . . to hear that you had wept
gave me hours of simple happiness.

NOT LOVE

Summer dusks, sunglare planing the back
    door, off-white paint curling
into flakes, fine ash, the wood weather-
    worn and almost hieroglyphic, I lift
the potted plant, night-blooming cereus
    flown east by a lover now distant,
and prop it on the warm stone steps
    so the sheaths might ease
upward and each leaf bathe in deepening
    glow. And grow. I tilt
water brimming the lip of a coffee can
    onto loose, black soil, then spoon
what pools from the saucer. Such tender-
    ness for these green yearnings,
slips whose only desire seems to be
    to awaken into final simplicity.
Urge and urge and urge, yawped Whitman.
    I want to awaken when the cereus
flowers to clip one cold blossom
    before it fails and press it between
ragged leaves of the 1892 "Death-Bed" edition
    for that woman I couldn't love
long enough, and for whom, not loving,
    I began to perfect these small,
sacramental gestures so that whatever tendril
    flourished between us might still
thrive, and her gift, however fragile,
    transmuted from the physical
world to the rough language of the text,
    might, after death, survive.

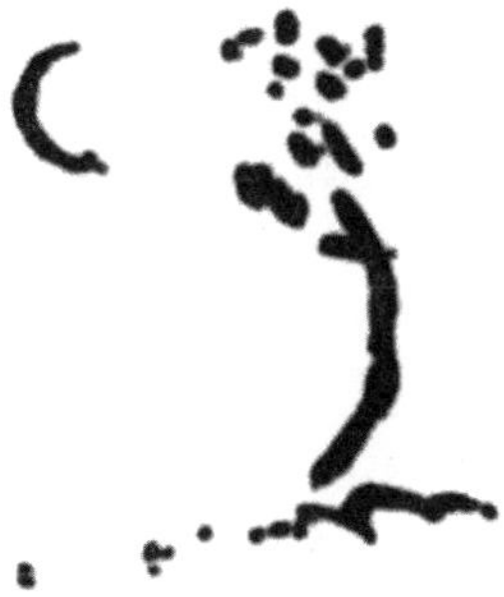

FIRST LESSON: WINTER TREES

These winter trees charcoaled against bare sky,
   a few quick strokes on the papery
      blankness, mean to suggest the mind
   leaping into paper, into sky, not bound
by the body's strict borders. The correspondence
   school instructor writes: *The ancient*
      masters loved to brush the trees
   in autumn, their blossoms fallen.
I've never desired the trees' generous
   flowering, but prefer this austere
      beauty, the few branches nodding
   like . . . like hair swept over a sleeping
lover's mouth, I almost thought too fast.
   Soon enough these patient alders
      will begin to blossom in their wild
   unremembering to inhabit the jade,
celebratory personae of late summer.
   So the task is simple: to live
      without yearning, to kindle
   this empty acre with trees touched
by winter, to shade them without simile,
   without strain. There: the winter trees.
      Their singular, hushed sufficiency.
Again. Again. Again. Again. Again.
Now you may begin to sketch the ceaseless winter rain.

CHRISOMS

early 19th C

Impossible curls fluorescing like aurorae,
    salmon limbs almost bursting with fat,
        they float in some ecclesiastical ether
    within cracked tondi darkened with rot.
God smiles upon them, and each smiles back.
    Smallpox, influenza, whooping cough, pleurisy,
        the simple wasting away in that snow-struck
    century—yet who's more joyous than twelve
chrisoms still swaddled in birth-clouds,
    the baptismal frocks that rendered them
        legless, half-spirit, while propped
    in doll-sized coffins, shed now as they rush
across the broad-brushed sky? Pure flesh
    lends symmetry: hibiscus buds of penises,
        the creamy, vaginal erasures
    babe-sweet, nimbus-wisped, incorruptible.
Good artists loathed them, so painted them
    with ferocity. Not one looks real, though.
        Not one seems the object of compassion
    or, for all such pious preening, envy.
While these dead daughters and sons remain
    perfect, ascendant, the planet
        still swerves, avoiding the sun.
    Chrisoms swarm the plains and beckon.
When we squint to name them, they're gone again.

EPHRATA

*An austere community of celibates founded in
Pennsylvania in 1732 by Johann Conrad Beissel,
Ephrata is an alternate name for Bethlehem.*

Who will name her now, our never-to-be-born,
    ghost orchid, hermit thrush,
        hedge-bindweed whose vine
    twirls only counterclockwise?

Is she sleeping on a splintery plank,
    poplar block for her pillow,
        seven celibate sisters
    crooning *Take away, take away sorrow?*

Or is she boarding the orphan train
    in the previous century's last
        snowstorm, clutching a letter
    in language no one can translate?

Let her gaze without fear into Jacob
    Riis's camera before the locomotive
        plunges west. Let her bathe
    in the baptismal waters of Ephrata.

Now you & I clutch each other,
    bundled in our grief, naming
        each winter constellation
    wheeling over the icy path—

Cassiopeia   The Pleiads—then together
begin to revise the stars:
       Blown Milkweed   Ragged Heart
Eighth Sister   Elizabeth

AVESTA

God's sparrow blown from its branch in the storm
splits open upon the mole-riddled lawn.
Her nest still tumbles among the yellow
horsemint and false nettle. Her nestlings lie
broken, transparent. Zoroastrians
take solace in a multiplicity
of souls, leaving cadavers exposed but
fettered so that no bone might be scattered,
missing on the day of resurrection.
Here in suburbia I let these birds
loose their odor of rot beyond the oak.
But I scoop up their nest, almost weightless,
to find—months after you've gone—coppery hairs
tendriling twigs and scraps of yarn, uncial,
some woven fragment of the sacred text:
Ahura Mazda requiring good deeds
to aid in his struggle against evil.
Light combs through the residual moisture,
illuminating souls that inhabit
ciphers of feather, eggshell, scavenged lock.
You'd prowled the deck that solstice dawn, naked
except for slashed panty hose, allowing
our neighbors, stunned over coffee, to stare
as you savaged your incandescent hair,
scissors crazed like some Hitchcockian flock.
The nest crumbles now into filaments
encircling my hand, your footfall almost
audible in each shorn, familiar strand.

NEW HOPE

The unforeseeable future, your absence assuming
  texture, arrives this October dusk
against the glass doors with such force, rainwater
  striking revisions upon the panes,
that the blown landscape, half-acre of ragged
  grasses, wavers & blurs, the evergreens
showering their thousand, combustible needles
  across the rotted planks of the deck.
Tomorrow I'll sweep away these clumped splinters
  to find among sap-clotted cones & papery
wasps' nests the scattered shards of the red
  & yellow hummingbird feeder, fiery
puzzle, each gaudy fragment the shape of a state
  we drove through, inch by mile,
to imagine our lives bound beyond the country
  inns & heaped breakfast trays,
beyond the exhaustion of AAA maps.
  This was your gift, not the beckoning
feeder or ceaseless, brassy chimes, but the quick
  dissolution of our plotted landscapes
for the sake of a central clarity: you & I
  in a pencil-post bed in some eighteenth-
century manor overlooking the Delaware River,
  trapped in the irony, one trip, of a town
named New Hope, the feeder unwrapped & dangling
  from the mirror, doubled brilliance
among crumpled newspaper wads. That last weekend
  a sudden squall funneled down the Gap,
alarming the Sunday boaters, couples racing
  both banks back to musty rooms, the far

shore barely visible from our balcony, but
    someone still there, perhaps a child,
calling, over & over, in a dying caterwaul
    muffled by foam, what sounded like your name.

MORRIS GRAVES: BLIND BIRD, 1940

Afterwards, I "took refuge" in books, reading
    even *The Road Less Traveled*, ignoring the wind
chimes' careless trill, the hummingbirds' peripheral
    beckonings. The VCR flashed its maddening
12:00 12:00 12:00 &, one dusk, the egg timer,
    its dispirited peep, startled me awake. On my lap
the catalog of the exhibit we'd viewed
    one blustery afternoon, the only two
touring the Wadsworth Atheneum, Graves' rough-hewn
    creatures helpless with desire.
I stared into his *Blind Bird*, gouache & watercolor:
    a lump of coal the earth refused to pressure
into something more exquisite; black pear
    abandoned in a previous century's still life—
the artist shut the attic door in despair,
    tossing her broken brushes away; hunched soul
tethered by talons to the clumped effluvia
    crisscrossing the empirical paths of the planet;
that most homely orchid, *Spiranthes lanceolata.*
    I swam in the pale wash of the portrait.
Blind bird, the obsidian eggs of your eyes rocked
    on their axes but returned nothing, not even
the thorny knowledge risen through neurons of mealy
    marrow to slake the thirst of the plump,
black pearl of your brain. I imagined the brief, wary
    flutterings; the uncommon kindnesses
of children who combed hair from their mothers'
    silver brushes to bolster you high
on the blossoming hydrangea above the wicked
    boys & prowling cats. Blind bird,
you slept with diamond-like intensity
    on mulberry paper. In our common dream,

our perpetual ache, your charred, smudged
        feathering begins its Pentecostal
healing as, slowly, you transfigure!—apricot
        & sleek, brassy whistler
anxious to fly, in the process of becoming
        1941's *Little Known Bird of the Inner Eye*.

THE CURIOSITIES

Medical Museum
Walter Reed Hospital

One jar stamped "what remains of the brain of Charles Guiteau"
& wedged among larger jars of pale microcephalics—
bug-eyed incubi squatting on sleepers in fairy-tale illustrations—
glints in the fluorescence. Stillborn
cyclops, syphilitic penises like blanched stalks of angelica,
the head of a young seaman flowering with red algae—
how would Whitman have catalogued this library
as he browsed hand-in-hand with his brakeman
among the singular stacks? Could his unshakable love
for the disinherited and homesick and gangrenous
teenage privates embrace these fused twins, their incestuous
union, face-trunk-crotch merging vertically
into crotch-trunk-face, blunt arms
radiating, little human starfish? My own lover
stares, rapt, at the stitched lips of these spongy children
who stare back from their brackish
cradle through decades of dust. Blistery nights,
as she twists in sleep, I'll slip off the sheet
& draw my fingers over her damp,
imperfect breasts till the dawn seeps outward,
till desire flares. How then can I forget
these jars stuffed with the invisible
masses who touch us in our dreams, who steep
our yearnings in their milky waters?—suspended
curiosities, terrible beauties, hushed assassins.

VOYEUR

His wife lay in bed, ungarlanded & huge, only days away from
    her long labor,
pierced by the single arrow of light the reading lamp cast:
Jeanne d'Arc allowing the lice-ridden straw heaped in her cell
to muffle, while she slept, the vigilant voices
promising Jesus' face—His kingdom come—for her brief,
    reluctant martyrdom:
bound feet rendered charred rubble, flames tonguing each
    nipple,
bored soldiers lustful now & the citizenry of Rouen jeering.
But these were his thoughts as he passed their window
led by the leashed dog, & his unbidden rage thickened the
    underbrush
into a ruttish buck, startled, needling his shoulder with such
    speed & power
he felt God-chastened, then utterly alone.
The retriever quivered, still tense, one more bestial synapse
    sparked;
through diamonds of lead-seamed glass he watched his wife
    shudder, their daughter within her
shuddering too; & because his mind would not shut itself,
remembered their drapes had again been left open on the night
    of conception,
their lovemaking self-conscious, a rehearsed choreography of
    mouths & genitals
for the imaginary voyeur who quickened their pleasure with his
    presence.

Ssss

Hush, hush . . . the twilight deepens with repetition
as her nipple slips from the milk-rimmed mouth,
and she exhales once more, *hush*,
this simple language of oceans cooling continents,
the *shhh* of creation
whispered by the smaller ocean of the amniotic sac
where the unborn floated, breather-to-be
who, after the slippery eruption into winter,
intuits that lost world from lips pressed by one finger
as the nursery door shuts, and so sleeps . . .

till beckoned, this evening, by creation's undersong
whistling its zero along the spine
flake by flake, until the whole skull glints
and snaps awake, *ssss*
burrowing deeper into marrow than its sister-sound, so
the infant clings, eyes struck open, to whichever Eve,
whichever Adam rushes to its night cry
to latch the window, feather the needled flesh,
soothe the hunched soul with a lullabye. *Hush* . . .
but the infant hears, beyond breath, dolls seething in the shadows.

SNOW GLOBE

In the miniature dome that holds my daughter
    beyond her bath- and story-time hour
(stocking stuffer from the mother
    who broods this Christmas without her),
the matchstick girl in patchwork frock
    clings to a lamppost, forever
wishing her frantic father might motor past
    to spot her among last-minute shoppers.
Tucked-in children love this tale, its simple
    lessons of trust and salvation, of never
giving over to the planet's vast despair.
    So the shivering soul remains stuck there.
But won't she drown? worries my daughter.
    No. She's taught herself to breathe in water.
Then with one quick twist of her wrist
    she tips the globe over, then back,
so a storm of glitter begins to swirl
    above blown braids of the luckless
girl, the false sleet flaring
    aurorae, an icy crown, till
foaming down over rag-bound feet
    as I'm struck by the terrible fact:
this daughter's element's not water. It's grief.
    And our little matchstick girl has drowned.

BURNING THE DOLLS

*In 1851, in John Humphrey Noyes' free-love
settlement in Oneida, New York, the commu-
nally-raised children, encouraged by the adults,
voted to burn their dolls as representative of the
traditional role of motherhood.*

That last night, unable to sleep,
    I prayed with my doll
        under the twisted-star
quilt, then held her close,

her flannel gown warming my cheek,
    her hair made of yarn
        brushing the tears away.
I sang her favorite lullaby,

then she sang it back to me.
    When the sky flared into dawn
        I carried her in my arm—
not crying now for anyone to see—

to my sisters barefoot on the lawn,
    circling the stacked wood, each
        bearing some small body
that stared into the remote sun.

And when the burning was done,
    when her white, Sunday dress
        was transformed to ash
and each perfect, grasping

finger melted upon the coals,
    when her varnished face burst
        in the furnace of my soul,
the waxy lips forever lost,

then I knew I'd no longer pray,
    even with fire haunting me,
        because I hadn't resembled
closely enough my mother,

hadn't withheld my burgeoning
    desire, so like a doll
        concealing what I'd learned
I burned and burned and burned.

SNOW CONE

Her tongue mimicked the color of her bikini
    after she'd licked the cherry
        snow cone, & the tip of the paper cup
    dripped fluorescent beads of syrup,
cool pinpricks, onto her oiled belly,
    the electric swirl pooling her pierced
        navel where the gold ring flashed.
    I told her its glittering would attract
sharks, how a novice scuba diver
    skimming the reef off the Caribbean
        coast of Costa Rica—I smiled at her—
had been taken headfirst into the maw
of a six-foot mako & blamed the attack
    on the cluster of studs rimming one ear.
        He'd managed to tear free & flail wildly
    to shore. Here I stroked her plaited hair.
The scars raking his skull seemed tribal,
    hewn in some Land-That-Time-Forgot coming-of-age
        ritual, but the raw stubs of his lobes
    oozed a milky gel that caked his cheeks.
As she jerked her braised shoulders
    in a tableau of revulsion, undone
        straps whisking sand, the icy
flavor overflowed her belly button,
ruby rill snaking toward her tan-line,
    then under the rim of triangular cloth.
        She gazed at me now, propped on both
    elbows, the snow cone like a splintery bulb
generated by body heat, its slow leak
    shape-shifting her pubis into a relief
        map of a savvy Third World country
    that exports slashed fins for soup

but saves, for the occasional tourist
    blundering through the market square
        in search of a cheap souvenir,
    the sun-bleached, primeval hoops of teeth.

WHITEFISH

Six months a year she worked in Cordova, in the fishing
    industry, sharing a trailer with five women.
Twelve-hour shifts six days a week, three cots in the trailer:
the day shift would stumble home to collapse into the still-warm
    bedding of the women leaving for night shift.
An endless succession of comings and goings, the Saturday day
    shift needing boyfriends to help home from the bars that
    night, the night shift needing their cots at Sunday dawn.
No work till six on Sunday when the shifts switched.
"The rest of the week the women would rather sleep than fuck,"
    she told me, "and besides it wasn't easy
to go home with men who joked about your fingers, the blood-
    rimmed nails, the smell even fresh lemons—you wouldn't
    believe the price—couldn't conceal.
But the money was good, only Saturday night booze to waste it
    on, unless your cowboy was a big spender,
and a few dozen air-freighted lemons."

But it's the work I remember more than the life, how she stood
    in the fluorescent glare,
the scaled fish scudding down a chute onto the glass table.
One by one she tweezered worms from their flesh, dropping them
    onto the concrete
until the floor seemed alive with long, threadlike, lipstick-red
    worms,
until the worms buried her boot-bottoms and she took a hose
    hanging from the ceiling and washed them into a trench
    along one wall.
"Someone shoveled them away between shifts, or burned them
    with lime, or packaged them for protein, who wanted to
    know?

Whitefish . . . ," she recoiled, mostly haddock for fish'n'chips
shops, the missed worms chopped and frozen and shipped,
then thawed and breaded and deep-fried, impossible to
recognize.
The worms came from the feces of dolphins who swallowed
garbage tossed from ships—whitefish nibbled the feces.

Our lovemaking was tentative, uneasy. I slept only in brief
intervals.
She'd been traveling for months, and we'd met in a tropical
climate,
but her fingers felt dead on my flesh, and though there was no
trace of blood or fishy odor, and she was a beautiful woman,
beautiful,
she had stood against a table in a flood of light in a bunker with
rows of women wearing black rubber boots,
all of them silent, all of them working their tweezers, the worms
writhing
until someone couldn't stand it another minute and took down
the hose to blast them back
while fish kept skidding down the chute and the next shift
awoke in their borrowed cots.

⁊

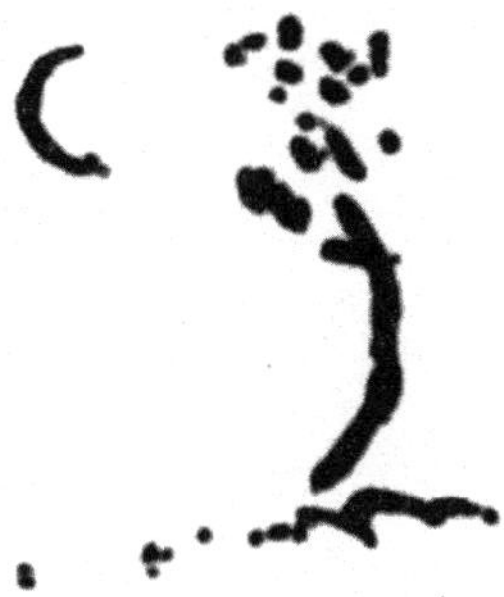

FIRST MILE

Not much of a challenge to anyone
    who'd spent winter tripling laps at the Y,
        but crossing Lake Forgotten dock to dam
    seemed an apt test at the time, so we dove,
then spoke as we eased past fanned pads, in shade,
    stroking the lake's slithery underskin.
        Our talk turned intimate—your arms flashing
    above that mirror, braceleted with weed,
beckoned me as I slowed in your wake,
    spuming *uh-huh* in response to my name.
        At the dam we hauled ourselves up
    onto the stone ledge to rest, brushing
hands and thighs, and the promise unspoken
    in any green romance dazzled in spindrift
        shaken from your hair. Who
    wouldn't be stunned, balanced on that lip
between pent-up seepage and nowhere,
    the drop-off to the umbrage
        steep, leaving us no choice
    as we sidled off moss
to begin the slippery mile back?
    But I grew weak, our cadence ceased
        as you surged ahead in your own fatigue
    till you lay toweled on the dock
watching me crawl the lake, dog-paddling,
    floating now on my back, anything
        to worry me closer to the ladder.

RAIN: LAKE FORGOTTEN

Fairy-fall,
the glaze of the peripheral
burnishes the barley, the bees' cuneiform
acrobatics in their collective flight home,
wherever home may be, under what eave or rafter or
in what box belonging to what keeper whose honey-borrowings,
in exchange for cloister, nurture whatever future
quivering antennae might foresee—
schemata of late spring
unwinding

◆

as lovers breaststroke
lake-lip to lake-ledge, pausing
to whisper among the floating pads or brush
thighs in the constant winnowing of water to stay
afloat, to drift together. The rain barely touches the lake's skin.
One voice, somnolent, dazes from speakers slung across
shoulders leaning toward the lake on the bridle
path from the barn. When the rain fails
to invisibility, the song will drone
the distances, tunneling the ids

◆

of lovers hauling themselves up now
onto a muck-slick verge where they will kneel
to shimmy down each other's suits and tongue the viscous
sugars iced there . . . while the schemata of late spring
require helpless, unself-conscious burrowings
toward such a future as we might make
in the light falling through rain
failing on the milky swans'-
wings of shattered
water

◆

as each sex-sopped lover lunges cleanly into the lake.

STONING THE BIRDS

How can any bird-hunting boy know the low passages
    through the thorned and knotted brambles
        till he veers off the horse trail
to startle some couple lovemaking among the pines,

her yessing head haloed with gnats as his back
    sweeps their splintery bed of brown
        needles, tongues looping their vague
script upon sky? I swayed near the thicket,

fingering pocketfuls of stones, till she stopped
    oaring the air to glance at me, register
        my familiar, acned face, then shrug
back to her sleepy summer pleasure. What did I matter,

one goofy teenager dumbstruck in khaki shorts,
    as he bucked and she bounced, then
        unglued herself from his glistening,
slug-slick stump? I finally jolted awake enough

to sneaker back the path to Twin Mountains Manor
    where my bent father swept long-legged
        spiders off the shuffleboard court
and my mother staggered the stiff-backed

Adirondack chairs into rows for spectators.
    I dawdled till the sinners sidled
        among us, staring hard for any sign
of dark complicity, tick-ridden consciences,

ash streaking her temple or sulphur slitting
    his eyes, as he chalked his name, *Benny*,
        onto the scoreboard, then toed the line.
What did I know about the fall of sunlight and shade

that slow June afternoon as my skinny buddies
    cannonballed from the low board, as Benny
        skimmed the puck toward the inverted
pyramid and all his proud sisters squealed?

I clumped up the knoll to the kiddie-loud
    pool and dove, wishing I could remain
        underwater till summer was over,
hold my breath till the planet stopped whirling

long enough for me to grasp it with cupped hands,
    press it against my cheek to measure
        the snared pulse—poor stunned jay—then
shovel it back into blue air and watch it flicker away.

THE FLOATING WREATHS

That was one summer's roughhousing pleasure:
    the fathers dunking the dry or unwary
        whose parroty squawks of sudden shock
    mixed with cool coos at such breezy tonic.
Ice cubes splashed in red plastic tumblers.

Then McAssey, knowing mother couldn't swim,
    arced her lounge off the shallow end,
        the water only three feet deep,
    but Mother panicked, couldn't get footing,
so settled to the serious business of drowning.

I knelt over the pool and looked into her face
    staring back at mine through wavery
        inches, barely a shimmer
    between our lips, twin souls untethered
to drift icy blue passages. "Mother!" I cried,

while she gazed upward with such terrible longing
    through chlorinated water that bleached
        her eyes and made them weep,
    this woman dissolving in her own sorrow
and the fearful reflection of my floating face,

till McAssey reached down past black inner tubes
    wreathing the water to grasp her fanned hair
        and haul her back into this world,
    sons and daughters grown suddenly sober,
this world of such cruel invention, then laughter.

THE BROOCH

Some cruel entrepreneur glued jewels onto wings
to prevent their broad, papery flowering,
the ruby or sapphire or smoky opal hump
wedged in an oval frame, its frail gold chain
blunted with a pin, so the exotic beetle,
living brooch, could plod its strict loop.
Pinned to my mother's monogrammed blouse,
that insect circled her initial, *D*, endlessly,
one arm of a clock wild with sprung tension,
symbol of *time passing* in early Bergman.
Then Mother cushioned a fish bowl with confetti,
the exiled prince plush in his glass palace,
and though she sprinkled water and crushed matzoh,
the beetle soon rocked onto its burdened back.
For days it lay among shredded funnies
because she couldn't bear to pry the jewel
from the sleek carapace, snap the foreign skull,
couldn't touch the withered roach.
No one spoke its brittle, miniature corpse.
Then Grandmother, in her gruff, Old World manner,
crumbled what remained of that conversation piece
into soot, the blue-black powder backdrop now
for the gem that flamed in her furrowed palm:
her stuck-in-the-throat history of sifting ash
from unearthed sancta of charred flesh
till clasping one daughter's heirloom brooch.

HERBS

Nothing made palpable the fragrance of their simmering
so much as their names:
Take Away Sorrow, Little Sister of the Moon.

Gold-green waters shirred pale nimbi
above the pallet where the child lay dying
while seven aunts tented her head with skirts
and prayed her breathe the buttery fumes.

Quitapena . . . they called on the forest paths,
Hermanita de la Luna as they bent to their task . . .
till one autumn feast day the fever broke.

Sixty years later the herbs still simmer
in clay pots over an open fire
as she clasps her sachet to crush a few leaves—
Take Away Sorrow fragrant still,

Little Sister of the Moon
breathing back the whole continent
with the barely perceptible

sweetness of its name.

CHRIST AT THE APOLLO, 1962

"Even in religious fervor there is a touch of animal heat."
—Walt Whitman

Despite the grisly wounds portrayed in prints,
the ropy prongs of blood stapling His eyes
or holes like burnt half-dollars in His feet,
the purple gash a coked teenybopper's
lipsticked mouth in His side, Christ's suffering
seemed less divine than the doubling-over
pain possessing "the hardest working man."
I still don't know whose wounds were worse: Christ's brow
thumbtacked with thorns, humped crowns of feet spike-split—
or James Brown's shattered knees. It's blasphemy
to equate such ravers in their lonesome
afflictions, but when James collapsed on stage
and whispered *please please please*, I rocked with cold,
forsaken Jesus in Gethsemane
and, for the first time, grasped His agony.
Both rose, Christ in His unbleached muslin gown
to assume His rightful, heavenly throne,
James wrapped in his cape, pussy-pink satin,
to ecstatic whoops of fans in Harlem.
When resurrection tugs, I'd rather let
The Famous Flames clasp my hand to guide me
than proud Mary or angelic orders
still befuddled by unbridled passion.
Pale sisters foistered relics upon me,
charred splinter from that chatty thief's cross and
snipped thread from the shroud that xeroxed Christ's corpse,
so I can't help but fashion the future—
soul-struck pilgrims prostrate at the altar
that preserves our Godfather's three-inch heels
or, under glass, like St. Catherine's skull, *please*,
his wicked, marcelled conk, his tortured knees.

THE '66 METS

The El rattled past the Unisphere, skeletal,
the gristly webbing of some sea creature
left to bleach in the industrial
rain of Queens. The World's Fair was over.
The game called, we were thrown together
hip-to-hip to convey the deep
disinterest of commuters in one another's
lives, staring hard into the abandoned
thoroughfares of the future, not speaking.
But breathing. And one fan sidled up
to nestle his mouth in my hair, his beery
breath swabbing one ear, stiff prick
pressed into the damp hollow of my back,
passengers packed around us, yet distant,
a crowd in a photograph, the couplings
not clear.
              Until a small commotion broke
out, some guy with two boys in baseball
gear clinging to his belt
warning, *Back off, bud,* his palm against
the breather's chest, the onlookers
tense but making room as the express
drummed into Queens Plaza and the amateur
molester ghosted off into the gray,
steel anonymity of the girders.
                         Fifteen,
I was too dumbstruck to murmur thanks, still
too simple to grasp how desire
can bully the body, any body, that father
ashen too, knuckling his boys' bristly
scalps beneath their blue caps
as the doors hissed shut and the train

jerked away from the station
into the spattering April
drizzle, an outcry of sparks
bursting from under blunt wheels,
the long, frustrating season just begun.

WASPS

for my father

Dead C battery, souvenir lighter, spool of thread,
lipstick tube lacking a smudge of red:
we'd rummage junk drawers to fill the squares.
But the lost chessmen?—
they click against glass, black
bishops bidding me open the window,
wheedling a wary God to release them
to crusade for their king gone ahead to Jerusalem.

LAST JOKE

"Mike's not gonna like it," my mother warned
in nervous, perpetual undersong,
but he blundered forward, slurring the one
about high-tech robots swarming the course—
caddies, groundskeepers, roving bartenders—,
the club members pleased, but then complaining
when the glare off tin torsos spoiled their scores.
"So they painted them black," he couldn't stop—
I could see what was coming, almost flinched,
while my mother scoured my kitchen basin,
hoping to avoid some loveless display,
the return to our hushed, prickly routine—
"and next day seven of them phoned in sick."
He stood scrappy, blunt as oak, sore loser,
knowing I'd voted for Clinton, "for choice,"
for lifting the ban on queers in foxholes,
the idea of some kid not unlike me
fixing the unbroken economy
rubbing him raw. "Dad," I growled, "not funny."
Who could have guessed this joke would be his last?—
not that watery, offensive punch line,
but his classic, bug-eyed zinger—Gotcha!—
as I chipped more ice into his Dewar's,
charmed by the flawless, cornball delivery.
"Pit bulls," sputtered my mother, letting go
the steel wool. We seeded our half-acre,
scorched scrub lawn, tramped combed furrows till his heart
hammered him home, and wasn't my mother
right? I didn't like it, but didn't flinch—
not from those black robots, their unforeseen
consequences, nor from the crude, helpless

humor of my father who taught me how
to spread just enough shit upon this green,
incorrect, forever dying planet.

DRIFTWOOD

God's castoff sculpture on the lesser scale:
        forget the riven spines of mountain range or
                rubble-strewn calderas thrust above sea level.
        Been there, done that, He might sigh. And Who
would compete with His own stubborn creation
        wasting a century to spire a single cathedral?
        So He works quickly, having read trendy
        texts on the art of *not-thinking,* those Zen
tea salesmen who honor watchful ancestors
        by pouring ceremonial clouds of steeping
                leaves into tiny, ceramic cups, never
        spilling a drop. One tear brims God's wide eye.
(Severe storm warnings flash along the coast.)
        He has no ancestors due homage, none
                to offer Him some thorny branch of wisdom.
        So He allows His hands to begin their work,
oak after long-standing oak pared to a knobby
        stick, teeth-marked pencil, nubbed
                splinter, then begin again, till
        the coaxed wood issues forth its primeval
soul, the cacophonous score of the creation
        captured in grooves and gnarls. This jazzy
                combo of wind and rain—God's callused palm,
        His blunt right thumb—conjures now a tulle
fog beachcombers must part in order to touch
        what's been tossed along the littoral:
                these modest abrasions shape-shifting
        with sand fleas, this rank curvature,
the swirling grain's giddy abstractions
        beckoning the sidewise crabs who vex
                from one knotty installation to the next,
        stalk-eyed critics ragging this tidal

gallery of slathered grit, frothing *no Louise*
    Nevelson while God sips one more scotch.
        Philistines, He fumes, *why do I bother?*
    but He won't return to marble, won't ever
go back to clay—why repeat Himself?
    He knows the artist has no choice
        but to bumble forward, abandoning
    each failure as He abandoned the grand
gesture, these crumbling continents, God's juvenilia.

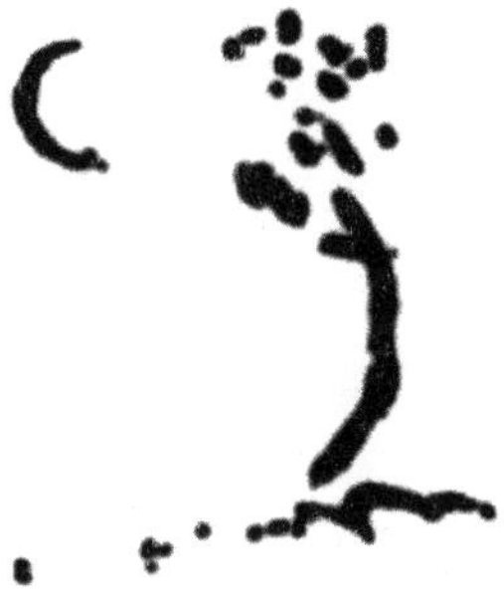

NOTES

"Parthenopi": The final version of the penultimate line may owe a slight debt to *Written on the Body* by Jeanette Winterson (New York: Alfred A. Knopf, 1993).

"New Age": *For J.*

"Simple Happiness": Henry James' remark to Whistler is recounted in *Whistler: Landscapes and Seascapes* by Donald Holden (New York: Watson-Guptill, 1976). Italo Svevo's letter, dated 23.12.1895, is reprinted in *Memoir of Italo Svevo* by Livia Veneziani Svevo, trans. Isabel Quigly (Marlboro, VT: The Marlboro Press, 1990).

"Not Love": *For KH*: Whitman's phrase appears in "Song of Myself."

"Avesta": *For T*: some lines suggested by the essay "Of Flaying, Dismemberment, and Other Inconveniences" in *Suspended Animation* by F. Gonzalez-Crussi (New York: Harcourt-Brace, 1995).

"The Curiosities": Charles Guiteau assassinated President James A. Garfield in 1881. According to Justin Kaplan in *Walt Whitman: A Life* (New York: Simon and Schuster, 1980): "In September 1871, at the invitation of the American Institute of New York, Whitman read in public a long poem ["After All, Not to Create Only"] he had composed for the opening of their annual industrial arts fair." The poem appeared in a dozen newspapers. "Congressman James Garfield, whom Walt frequently ran into along Pennsylvania Avenue, saluted him by raising his right arm and saying with a smile, '"After all, not to create only."'"

"Herbs": With gratitude to Sandra Fuensalida for the names of herbs in her native Chile.

"Christ at the Apollo, 1962": *For Andrew Hudgins*: The epigraph by Whitman is taken from his essay "Democratic Vistas" (1871); the poem was triggered, in part, by a conversation with novelist Richard Price who had once interviewed James Brown. At Price's request, the Godfather of Soul had hoisted his trousers to display his knees, damaged by years of dropping to the stage at the climax of his show.

"The '66 Mets": 1966: the year the Mets first rose from the cellar.

"Last Joke": *In memoriam Raymond Waters* d. August 14, 1993.

"Driftwood": *In memoriam Thomas Bellavance.*

ACKNOWLEDGMENTS

Grateful acknowledgment is made to the editors of journals in which these poems, often in earlier versions, first appeared:

The American Poetry Review: "Two Baths";

The American Voice: "Herbs," "Last Joke";

The Bellingham Review: "Swamp Rose Mallow," "Everlasting Pea";

Chelsea: "Chrisoms";

Cimarron Review: "Wasps";

Crazyhorse: "Simple Happiness," "Ssss";

The Georgia Review: "Parthenopi";

The Gettysburg Review: "Green Ash, Red Maple, Black Gum," "New Hope," "Driftwood";

The Illinois Review: "Airing the Mattress," "The Floating Wreaths";

the magazine (England): "Everlasting Pea";

Mississippi Review: "The Curiosities";

Mississippi Valley Review: "Whitefish," "Rain: Lake Forgotten";

The Missouri Review: "First Lesson: Winter Trees," "First Mile," "Stoning the Birds," "Christ at the Apollo, 1962," "The '66 Mets";

The North American Review: "New Age," "Snow Globe";

The Ohio Review: "God at Forty";

Ploughshares: "The Brooch";

Poetry: "Not Love";

Poetry Ireland Review: "Green Ash, Red Maple, Black Gum";

Salt Hill Journal: "Morris Graves: *Blind Bird*, 1940"; "Voyeur";

Seneca Review: "Burning the Dolls";

Southern Poetry Review: "Avesta".

"Green Ash, Red Maple, Black Gum" was reprinted as a limited edition pamphlet, with an etching by Lloyd Kelly, by the Fine Arts Center, Longwood College, Virginia, 1993.

"First Lesson: Winter Trees" was reprinted in *The Signature Series* #1 (Oneonta, NY: Catskill Poetry Workshop, Hartwick College, 1995).

"Last Joke" was reprinted in *The Signature Series* #2 (Oneonta, NY: Catskill Poetry Workshop, Hartwick College, 1996).

"Christ at the Apollo, 1962" was reprinted in *Sweet Nothings: An Anthology of Rock and Roll in American Poetry*, ed. Jim Elledge (Bloomington: Indiana University Press, 1994).

"Parthenopi" and "The Brooch" were reprinted in the 1995-1996 *Anthology of Magazine Verse & Yearbook of American Poetry*, ed. Alan F. Pater (Beverly Hills, CA: Monitor, 1997).

"Burning the Dolls" was reprinted in *Seneca Review: A 25th Anniversary Retrospective* and was included in *The Burden Lifters* (Pittsburgh, PA: Carnegie Mellon University Press, 1989).

I want to thank the Corporation of Yaddo, the MacDowell Colony, the Virginia Center for the Creative Arts, and the Tyrone Guthrie Centre (Ireland) for residency fellowships, and the Maryland State Arts Council for Individual Artist Awards.

The Salisbury State University Foundation, Inc., and the Fulton School of Liberal Arts at SSU offered generous support which enabled me to complete this book.

Thanks also to Joan Connor, Carol Frost, Jeffrey Skinner &, especially, Richard Foerster for their generous reading & suggestions, & to Gary Harrington for his friendship. And to my daughter, Kiernan, pure pleasure, I remain immeasurably grateful.

Excerpt from *Justine*, by Lawrence Durrell, copyright © 1957, renewed © 1985 by Lawrence George Durrell. Used by permission of Dutton Signet, a division of Penguin Books USA Inc.

Excerpt from *Pan*, by Knut Hamsun, translated by James W. McFarlane. Translation © 1957 by The Noonday Press. Copyright renewed © 1984 by Farrar, Straus & Giroux, Inc. Reprinted by permission of Farrar, Straus & Giroux, Inc.

ABOUT THE AUTHOR

Michael Waters is Professor of English at Salisbury State University on the Eastern Shore of Maryland. His previous volumes include *Bountiful* (1992), *The Burden Lifters* (1989), *Anniversary of the Air* (1985)—these titles from Carnegie Mellon University Press—*Not Just Any Death* (BOA Editions, 1979), and *Fish Light* (Ithaca House, 1975). Among his awards are a Fellowship in Creative Writing from the National Endowment for the Arts, two Individual Artist Awards from the Maryland State Arts Council, and two Pushcart Prizes. He has taught in the creative writing programs at Ohio University and the University of Maryland and has been Visiting Professor of American Literature at the University of Athens, Greece, as well as Banister Writer-in-Residence at Sweet Briar College in Virginia.

BOA EDITIONS, LTD.

AMERICAN POETS CONTINUUM SERIES

Vol. 1   *The Fuhrer Bunker: A Cycle of Poems in Progress*
W. D. Snodgrass

Vol. 2   *She*
M. L. Rosenthal

Vol. 3   *Living With Distance*
Ralph J. Mills, Jr.

Vol. 4   *Not Just Any Death*
Michael Waters

Vol. 5   *That Was Then: New and Selected Poems*
Isabella Gardner

Vol. 6   *Things That Happen Where There Aren't Any People*
William Stafford

Vol. 7   *The Bridge of Change: Poems 1974–1980*
John Logan

Vol. 8   *Signatures*
Joseph Stroud

Vol. 9   *People Live Here: Selected Poems 1949–1983*
Louis Simpson

Vol. 10   *Yin*
Carolyn Kizer

Vol. 11   *Duhamel: Ideas of Order in Little Canada*
Bill Tremblay

Vol. 12   *Seeing It Was So*
Anthony Piccione

Vol. 13   *Hyam Plutzik: The Collected Poems*

Vol. 14   *Good Woman: Poems and a Memoir 1969–1980*
Lucille Clifton

Vol. 15   *Next: New Poems*
Lucille Clifton

Vol. 16   *Roxa: Voices of the Culver Family*
William B. Patrick

Vol. 17   *John Logan: The Collected Poems*

Vol. 18   *Isabella Gardner: The Collected Poems*

Vol. 19   *The Sunken Lightship*
Peter Makuck

Vol. 20   *The City in Which I Love You*
Li-Young Lee

Vol. 21   *Quilting: Poems 1987–1990*
Lucille Clifton

Vol. 22   *John Logan: The Collected Fiction*

Vol. 23   *Shenandoah and Other Verse Plays*
Delmore Schwartz

Vol. 24   *Nobody Lives on Arthur Godfrey Boulevard*
Gerald Costanzo

Vol. 25   *The Book of Names: New and Selected Poems*
Barton Sutter

Vol. 26   *Each in His Season*
W. D. Snodgrass

Vol. 27   *Wordworks: Poems Selected and New*
Richard Kostelanetz

Vol. 28   *What We Carry*
Dorianne Laux

Vol. 29   *Red Suitcase*
Naomi Shihab Nye

Vol. 30   *Song*
Brigit Pegeen Kelly

Vol. 31   *The Fuehrer Bunker: The Complete Cycle*
W. D. Snodgrass

Vol. 32   *For the Kingdom*
Anthony Piccione

Vol. 33   *The Quicken Tree*
Bill Knott

Vol. 34   *These Upraised Hands*
William B. Patrick

Vol. 35   *Crazy Horse in Stillness*
William Heyen